First Facts®

Amazing Animal Arch

D0879416

AMAZING Animal Architects of the Water

A 4D BOOK

by Yvonne Pearson

Consultants:
James L. Gould
Professor
Department of Ecology and Evolutionary Biology
Princeton University

Carol Grant Gould
Science Writer
Princeton, N.J.

PEBBLE
a capstone imprint

Download the Capstone 4D app!

- Ask an adult to download the Capstone 4D app.
- Scan the cover and stars inside the book for additional content.

When you scan a spread, you'll find fun extra stuff to go with this book! You can also find these things on the web at www.capstone4D.com using the password: water.26837

First Facts are published by Pebble
1710 Roe Crest Drive, North Mankato, Minnesota 56003
www.mycapstone.com

Copyright © 2019 by Pebble, a Capstone imprint. All rights reserved. No part of this publication may be reproduced in whole or in part, or stored in a retrieval system, or transmitted in any form or by any means, electronic, mechanical, photocopying, recording, or otherwise, without written permission of the publisher.

Library of Congress Cataloging-in-Publication Data
Names: Pearson, Yvonne, author.
Title: Amazing animal architects of the water : A 4D book
  / by Yvonne Pearson.
Description: North Mankato, Minnesota : an imprint of Pebble, [2019] |
  Series: First facts. Amazing animal architects | Audience: Ages 6–8. |
  Includes index.
Identifiers: LCCN 2017057834 (print) | LCCN 2018002221 (ebook) | ISBN
  9781543526912 (ebook PDF) | ISBN 9781543526837 (hardcover) | ISBN
  9781543526875 (pbk.)
Subjects: LCSH: Animals—Habitations—Juvenile literature. | Animal
  behavior—Juvenile literature. | Aquatic habitats—Juvenile literature.
Classification: LCC QL756 (ebook) | LCC QL756 .P425 2018 (print) | DDC
  591.56/4—dc23
LC record available at https://lccn.loc.gov/2017057834

Editorial Credits
Karen Aleo, editor; Sarah Bennett, designer; Morgan Walters, media researcher;
Tori Abraham, production specialist

Photo Credits
Alamy: Chris Howarth/Chile, 19, Papilio, 13; Getty Images: Picavet, 9; Newscom: A. Hartl/ picture alliance / blickwinkel/A, 21, Dave Watts/NHPA/Photoshot, 17; Shutterstock: chakkrachai nicharat, 11, Chase Dekker, Cover, Chutima Chaochaiya, (blueprint) design element, Miloje, (grunge) design element, Natalia5988, (brush grunge) design element, Peter Hermes Furian, (map) design element, Remoau, 5, SARAWUT KUNDEJ, 15, Viktor Loki, 7

Printed in China.
000306

Table of Contents

Amazing Builders

Animals build amazing houses in or near the water. Some animals gather grass, stones, and sticks. Other animals make building materials inside their bodies. One animal uses its own body as the building material!

The homes they build keep the animals and their young safe. They can help protect the animals from **predators**.

predator—an animal that hunts other animals for food

Ducks may build nests on the ground where it is wet.

Beavers

How do beavers build their homes? First, many build a **dam**. They gnaw trees until they fall across streams. Then they pile branches, stones, and mud on the trees.

A dam helps make a pond still and safe for a beaver's **lodge**. The beavers build their lodges with wood, stones, and plants. They use mud to make their homes waterproof.

dam—a barrier built to block a body of water

lodge—a beaver's home of mud, logs, and sticks, built in the water

WHERE BEAVERS LIVE

Beaver dams are found in freshwater ponds and rivers. Beavers build a lodge close to the dam.

RANGE MAP

lodge

dam

Caddisflies

Caddisfly **larvae** build cases shaped like tiny tubes. They build the tubes using sand, stones, and snail shells. They make silk in their bodies that glue the materials together.

The cases protect the larvae as they grow. The stone cases also keep the larvae from being swept away in the water.

pronunciation: caddisfly (KAD-is-fly)

stone case

larva—an insect at the stage of development between an egg and an adult; more than one larva is called larvae.

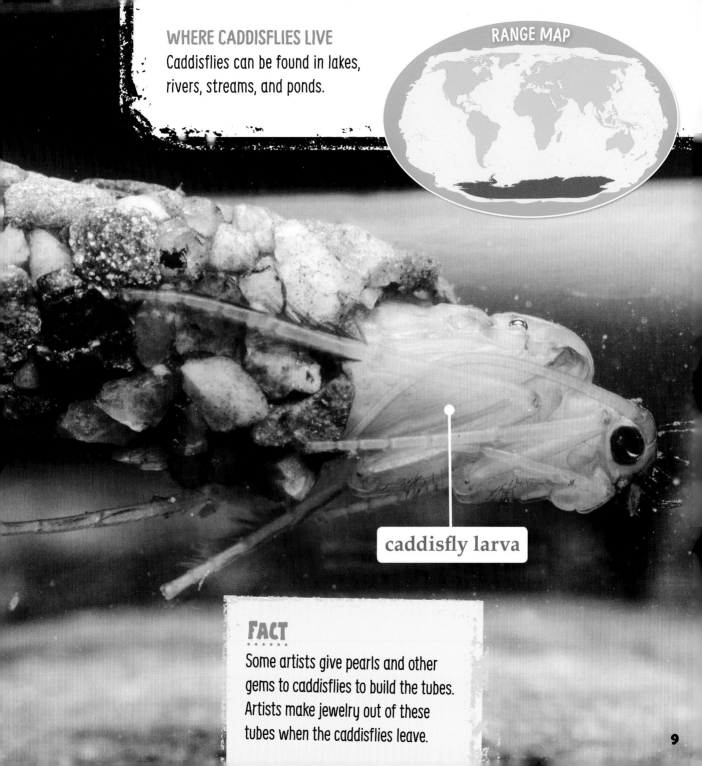

WHERE CADDISFLIES LIVE
Caddisflies can be found in lakes,
rivers, streams, and ponds.

RANGE MAP

caddisfly larva

FACT

Some artists give pearls and other
gems to caddisflies to build the tubes.
Artists make jewelry out of these
tubes when the caddisflies leave.

Fire Ants

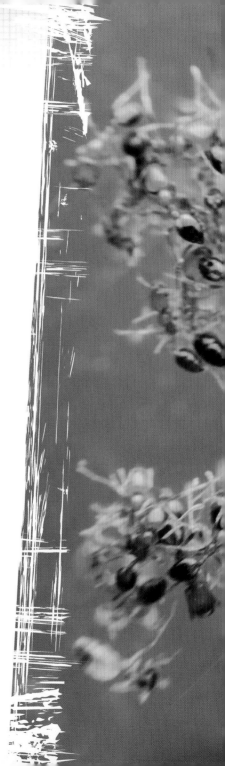

When there's a flood, fire ants keep their queen and larvae safe. They build rafts by linking their bodies together. In this way, they make sure their **colony** survives. They trap air bubbles to help them float. A material like wax helps keep them dry.

Fire ants can attack humans and animals. The ants have strong stings and powerful jaws.

colony—a large group of insects that live together

WHERE FIRE ANTS LIVE

Fire ants build mounds in sunny places. After a lot of rain, fire ants might be found floating in water.

RANGE MAP

Túngara Frogs

Túngara frogs keep their eggs safe in a nest made of bubbles. The female gives off liquid from her body on the water. The male holds onto her back. The male whips the liquid into bubbles with his back legs. Then the female lays eggs in the bubbles. The bubbles keep out predators and germs. They also keep the eggs from drying out.

pronunciation: túngara (toon-GAH-ra)

FACT
Frog foam may someday be used to keep harmful germs out of people's cuts.

WHERE TÚNGARA FROGS LIVE
Túngara frogs make nests in water on forest floors in hot places.

RANGE MAP

Corals

Coral reefs look like colorful underwater castles. They are really the **skeletons** of tiny **polyps**.

Each polyp makes a hard skeleton shaped like a cup. The polyp sits inside the cup to stay safe. Many polyps group together and form a reef.

skeleton—the bones that support and protect the body of a human or other animal

polyp—a small sea animal with a tube-shaped body

WHERE CORALS LIVE

Corals are found on sandy bottoms of warm oceans.

RANGE MAP

FACT

Corals are very important. They give shelter to one-fourth of ocean life.

Platypuses

Platypuses build **burrows** in riverbanks. They often find places where branches grow over the banks. The branches **camouflage** the entrances to their burrows.

When the female is ready to lay eggs, she digs a deep burrow. She lines it with wet leaves and grass to make it soft. She plugs the entrance with soil. This keeps the young safe from predators and floods.

burrow—a tunnel or hole in the ground made or used by an animal

camouflage—coloring or covering that makes animals, people, and objects look like their surroundings

WHERE PLATYPUSES LIVE
Platypuses build two kinds of burrows. One is to live in and the other is for nesting.

RANGE MAP

FACT

Platypuses look like they are part duck, part beaver, and part otter.

Horned Coots

Can a bird build an island? Horned coots can. They collect stones from the shore. Then they drop them one by one in a shallow part of a lake. The stones pile up to make a **dome** above the water. The birds cover the stones with **algae** to make a big nest. The island keeps the eggs safe from being washed away.

dome—a structure shaped like half of a ball

algae—small plants without roots or stems that grow in water or on damp surfaces

WHERE HORNED COOTS LIVE

Horned coots build nests in lakes high in the Andes Mountains.

RANGE MAP

FACT

A horned coot's island can weigh 1.5 tons (1.4 metric tons).

Sticklebacks

Male stickleback fish use a liquid from their bodies to make nests. The liquid causes plant parts to stick together. Then sticklebacks use their bodies to push the materials into a tunnel shape.

Females lay eggs in the tunnels. The females leave after laying eggs. Then the males take care of the eggs and young fish.

RANGE MAP

Glossary

algae (AL-jee)—small plants without roots or stems that grow in water or on damp surfaces

burrow (BUHR-oh)—a tunnel or hole in the ground made or used by an animal

camouflage (KA-muh-flahzh)—coloring or covering that makes animals, people, and objects look like their surroundings

colony (KAH-luh-nee)—a large group of insects that live together

dam (DAM)—a barrier built to block a body of water

dome (DOHM)—a structure shaped like half of a ball

larva (LAR-vuh)—an insect at the stage of development between an egg and an adult; more than one larva is called larvae.

lodge (LOJ)—a beaver's home of mud, logs, and sticks, built in the water

polyp (POL-ip)—a small sea animal with a tube-shaped body

predator (PRED-uh-tur)—an animal that hunts other animals for food

skeleton (SKEL-uh-tuhn)—the bones that support and protect the body of a human or other animal